Kidnap!

Angela Llanas

1 The letter

Ben and Mary Brown are ten-year-old twins. They live with their parents in an apartment on the top floor of a tall building. Their apartment is in the middle of the city.

The twins were on their long summer holiday. One day the postman brought a letter for Ben and Mary. Mary quickly opened it.

'Ben!' she shouted. 'It's from Uncle Tom and Aunt Jane.'

Ben put down his book. 'What do they say?' he asked.

'They have rented a house on the coast and say we can stay with them.'

'Let me see the letter,' said Ben. He read the letter. 'Uncle Tom has rented a boat too, so we can go fishing.'

'Yes,' said Mary. 'We can go swimming too. I hope Mom and Dad will let us go.'

'Me too,' said Ben. 'We'll ask them.'

Mary gave her mother the letter and Mrs. Brown read it.

'Can we go?' asked Mary.

'It's boring here in summer,' said Ben. 'There's nothing to do.'

'Can they stay with Tom and Jane?' said Mrs. Brown to her husband. 'It sounds like a good idea to me.'

'Why not? I think it's a great idea,' said Mr. Brown.

'You must be good,' said Mrs. Brown. 'You must help your aunt in the house.'

'Of course we'll help her,' said Mary. Ben didn't say anything because he doesn't like housework.

'Write to your uncle and aunt and tell them that you can go,' said Mrs. Brown.

The next day, Mary wrote the letter. Then she and Ben looked for their beach things. Their swimsuits were too small and their goggles were broken.

'The flippers are OK,' said Ben.

'Mine aren't,' said Mary. 'They're too small.'

'We'll have to buy new swimsuits, new goggles and new flippers,' said Ben.

'Let's go to the store,' said Mary.

'Do you have any money?' asked Ben.

'Yes,' said Mary. 'I've saved some of my birthday money.'

'Could you lend me some?' asked Ben. 'I don't have any.'

'I might,' said Mary. 'If you help Aunt Jane with the housework as well.'

'Oh, all right,' said Ben.

Mary and Ben went to the post office and mailed the letter. Then they went to the store. They bought new swimsuits and goggles. They bought some new flippers for Mary.

'I'm going to buy a present for Aunt Jane,' said Mary.

'And I'll buy a present for Uncle Tom,' said Ben. 'Can I have some money, please?'

Mary gave Ben some money. He bought a book on sailing.

'Uncle Tom will like this,' he said. 'He's rented a boat. He should read this book.'

'That's a good idea,' said Mary. 'I've bought a scarf for Aunt Jane. It's really beautiful. I'm sure she'll like it.'

Mary and Ben bought some film for their camera and then they went home.

'We've bought everything we need,' said Mary.

'I've spent all my money,' said Ben.

'You've spent all my money,' said Mary.

2 On the coast

A week later, Mary and Ben went to the coast by train. Mr. and Mrs. Brown took them to the station. Mrs. Brown bought some comics.

'You can read these on the train,' she said.

Mr. Brown bought some sweets and drinks.

Mary and Ben got on the train. A man waved a flag and the train began to move.

'Goodbye!' shouted Mary and Ben.

'Have a good time,' said Mrs. Brown. 'Remember to help your Aunt Jane. And don't forget to brush your teeth in the morning and at night.'

The train moved more quickly.

'Goodbye!' shouted Mr. and Mrs. Brown.

Three hours later, the train arrived at the coast, but Mary and Ben couldn't see the sea.

'Where's the sea?' asked Ben.

'I can't see it,' said Mary.

Uncle Tom and Aunt Jane were on the platform.

'Hi!' they said. 'Welcome to Sandy Bay!'

'Where's the sea?' asked Ben.

'Where's the house?' asked Mary.

'Is it near the sea?' said Ben.

'Do you have a big boat?' said Mary.

'Can we go fishing?' asked Ben.

'Wait a moment,' said Uncle Tom. 'You'll soon see everything.'

'Let's put your bags in the car,' said Aunt Jane. 'And we'll go to the house.'

The car stopped in front of the house. It was an old house and it was very small. There was a garden with a tall tree.

Ben looked at the tree.

'No, Ben,' said his uncle. 'You must not climb it. You'll break a leg and that will be the end of your holiday.'

'Come in,' said Aunt Jane. 'Your rooms are in the attic.'

The rooms were small, but they had windows. Ben went to the window of his room. He looked out.

'Come here, Mary,' he shouted.

Mary and Ben looked out of the window. They could see the garden. They could see the beach and they could see the sea.

'It's great!' said Ben happily.

'I can see a boat on the beach. Look!' said Mary.

Mary and Ben had their lunch.

'Now I'll take you to the boat,' said Uncle Tom. It was a small boat, but it had a big white sail.

'Great!' said Ben. 'Can we go for a ride now?'

'Yes. Let's go,' said Uncle Tom. 'The weather is good. There is a wind so it's a good day for sailing.'

Mary and Ben ran to the boat and climbed in. Then Aunt Jane got in. Uncle Tom pushed the boat into the sea and he jumped in too.

'Put these on,' said Aunt Jane.

'What are they?' asked Ben.

'They're life jackets,' said Uncle Tom. 'We always wear them in case the boat turns over.'

3 The big boat

The boat sailed out to sea. Uncle Tom taught the children how to move the sail and steer the boat. Then they saw a large boat with very big white sails.

'Can you see that boat?' said Uncle Tom. 'It belongs to the East family.'

'It's very big,' said Ben. 'Are they rich?'

'Yes,' said Aunt Jane. 'They are very rich. They have a big house with a swimming pool. You can see it from here.' She pointed to a big white house.

'Do they have any children?' asked Mary.

'Yes, they have a boy,' said Uncle Tom, 'but he's a little younger than you. His name is Peter.'

'Let's go back,' said Aunt Jane. 'I'm cold.'

The boat sailed back to the beach. Uncle Tom and the children pulled it out of the water. Uncle Tom took the sail off the boat.

'Look,' said Ben. 'The big boat is coming in too.'

'It isn't coming to the beach,' said Uncle Tom. 'It's going to the marina. The big boats stay in the marina.'

'Let's go and see the big boats,' said Ben.

'I must clean the boat,' said Uncle Tom.

'I must cook our dinner,' said Aunt Jane.

'Can we go to the marina?' asked Ben.

'Yes,' said Aunt Jane, 'but don't be late for dinner.'

Mary and Ben went to the marina. There were a lot of big boats in the marina.

The Easts' boat came in. Three people were on the boat. One was a tall man, wearing a uniform. He sailed the boat. One was a big man. He was Mr. East. It was his boat.

'He's rich,' said Ben. 'I'm going to be rich and have a big boat.'

'There's the boy,' said Mary. 'That must be Peter.'

The boy was about eight years old. He had a fishing rod and a big fish.

'He's caught a fish,' said Ben.

Mr. East and his son got off the boat. A big car drove up to them and stopped.

'Look!' said Ben. 'They have a big car as well.'

'And a man to drive it,' said Mary.

'I'm going to have a big car,' said Ben. 'But I'm not going to have a driver. I want to drive the car.'

The driver got out of the car and opened the trunk. He put the boy's fishing rod and the fish in the trunk. Then he opened the door for Mr. East and his son. He closed the door, got into the car and drove towards the big white house.

A man took a photo of the car.

'Did you see that man?' asked Mary. 'He took a photo of the car.'

The man got into a small car and drove away.

'I saw him,' said Ben. 'He was hiding behind some boxes. He didn't want to be seen. He took a lot of photos of Mr. East and his son.'

'I wonder why he took the photos?' said Mary.

'I don't know,' said Ben. 'Perhaps he works for a newspaper.'

'Why did he hide behind the boxes?' said Mary.

'I don't know,' said Ben. 'Did you see his face?'

'Yes,' said Mary. 'He looks evil. I don't like him. I think he's a bad man.'

'I'm hungry,' said Ben. 'Look at the time! It's late and I want my dinner.'

'OK,' said Mary. 'We mustn't be late for dinner. Let's go back to the house.'

The next morning, Mary got up at seven o'clock and looked out of her window. She went to her brother's room.

'Ben,' she said.

'What is it?' said Ben sleepily. 'What's the matter?'

'Come with me,' said Mary.

The children went to the window.

'Can you see that man?' asked Mary.

'Where?' said Ben.

'He's behind that rock,' said Mary.

'I can see him now,' said Ben. 'I know him. We saw him yesterday.'

'Yes,' said Mary. 'It's the man who was at the marina. He took photos of Mr. East and his son.'

'What is he doing now?' asked Ben.

'I don't know,' said Mary. 'Perhaps he's taking more photos.'

4 The detectives

The man came from behind the rock and walked towards the marina.

'I'm going to follow him,' said Ben.

'Be careful,' said Mary.

Ben went down the stairs and Mary watched through the window. Ben came out of the house and ran through the garden to the beach. He walked along the beach.

The man walked along the road. Then he stopped and turned to look at the beach so Ben quickly hid behind a rock.

Then Ben saw another man. He was the sailor from Mr. East's boat. The two men talked for a few minutes. Ben listened, but he couldn't hear the men.

The sailor went towards the marina. The other man went towards the village so Ben followed him.

The man went into a small hotel. Ben waited near the hotel for an hour, but the man did not come out so Ben went home.

'Hello, Ben,' said his aunt. 'Where have you been?'

'I've been to the village,' said Ben.

His aunt put his breakfast on the table. Ben was very hungry after his walk.

After breakfast, Ben and Mary went into the garden. Ben told Mary about the man.

'He talked to the sailor,' he said.

'What are they going to do?' said Mary.

'I don't know,' said Ben. 'Perhaps they are going to rob Mr. East. He's very rich.'

'But the sailor works for Mr. East,' said Mary. 'The other man is watching Mr. East and he's watching his house too.'

'Shall we tell Mr. East about them?' asked Ben.

'I don't know,' said Mary. 'Perhaps we are wrong.'

'Shall we tell Uncle Tom?' asked Ben.

'No,' said Mary. 'Let's play detectives.'

'OK,' said Ben. 'I'm Sherlock Holmes and you're Doctor Watson.'

Ben and Mary went to the beach and Ben pointed to a rock.

'The man was there,' he said. 'Let's go to the rock.'

Ben and Mary went to the rock.

'Yes,' said Ben. 'I can see the big white house from here.'

'What shall we do?' said Ben.

'Nothing,' said Mary. 'I don't want to play detectives any more. I'm bored. I prefer collecting shells. Let's collect some shells.'

'I prefer being a detective,' said Ben.

Mary and Ben went home. Ben looked at the tall tree.

'If I climb the tree, I can see the beach,' he said.

'I'm going to collect some shells,' said Mary.

Ben climbed the tall tree. He could see Mary on the beach. She collected some beautiful shells. Then she walked towards the marina. Suddenly, she stopped. She saw the sailor. He was near Mr. East's boat. He looked at his watch. Mary sat on the sand and watched the sailor.

'She's playing detectives again,' said Ben.

Mary waited on the beach.

Then Mr. East's car came. It stopped at the marina and the driver got out. He opened the back door and Peter got out.

'Are we going fishing?' asked Peter.

The driver didn't answer. He got into the car and drove off.

'Let's go fishing,' said Peter to the sailor.

'In a minute,' said the sailor. 'We're waiting for somebody.'

Another car came. It was a small red car. It stopped and a man got out.

5 The kidnapping

The man went to Peter.

'Come with me,' he said. He took Peter's hand and pulled him to the small car.

'I don't want to go,' shouted Peter. 'I'll tell my father.'

The man pushed the boy into the car. Mary stood up and ran to the men.

'Stop!' she shouted. 'Let him go!'

'Where did she come from?' said the man.

'I don't know,' said the sailor. 'But we'll have to take her too.'

The sailor took Mary's hand and pushed her into the car, next to Peter. The men jumped into the car and quickly drove away.

Ben was in the tall tree and he saw everything. He climbed down the tree and ran to the house.

'Uncle Tom!' he shouted. 'Come quickly!'

'What's the matter?' asked Uncle Tom.

'Two men have kidnapped Mary,' he said. 'And they've kidnapped Peter East too!'

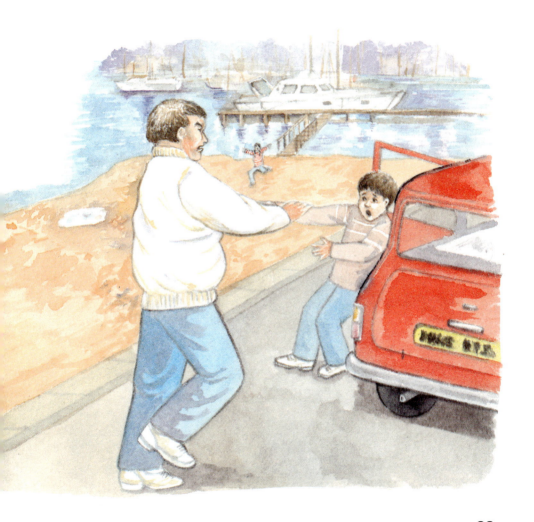

'What happened?' said Uncle Tom.

'I was up in the tall tree,' said Ben. 'Mr. East's car arrived at the marina, Peter got out and the driver left. Then a little red car came. A man was in it. He put Peter East in his car. Mary tried to stop him, so the sailor put her in the car too! Mary was crying.'

'What was the car like?' asked Uncle Tom.

'It was a small red car,' said Ben.

'Did you see the license plate number?' asked Uncle Tom.

'I can remember the last three numbers,' said Ben. 'They were 3-6-7.'

Uncle Tom phoned the police, told them about the kidnapping and described the car. Then Uncle Tom and Ben got into their car.

'Perhaps we can catch them,' said Uncle Tom. 'They went along this road, didn't they?'

'Yes,' said Ben.

Uncle Tom saw the small red car. It was in front of a big house. Uncle Tom stopped and got out of the car.

'Stay here, Ben,' he said. 'The men might be dangerous.'

Uncle Tom ran to the house. He looked through a window. It was the kitchen. The men were in the room. They were talking. Uncle Tom couldn't see Mary or Peter. He ran back to his car.

'I'm going to phone the police again,' he said.

Two police cars arrived with sirens screaming. The cars stopped and the policemen jumped out.

'The men are in the kitchen,' said Uncle Tom. 'I don't know where the children are.'

Three policemen ran to the front door of the house and three went to the back door. The policemen rushed into the house. Five minutes later they came out with the two men. Mary and Peter were with them, too.

'Are you all right, Mary?' asked Uncle Tom.

'I'm fine, thanks,' said Mary. She was a brave girl. 'Peter is fine, too.'

A policeman came up to Uncle Tom. 'I've questioned the men,' he said. 'They say they kidnapped Peter East because they wanted a lot of money for him. They took Mary because she tried to stop them. She was very brave.'

Peter East got into a police car and the police took him home. Mary and Ben got into Uncle Tom's car. He drove them home.

Aunt Jane was very happy. 'I was very worried,' she said. 'I telephoned your mother and father. They are coming.'

'When are they coming?' asked Mary.

'This afternoon,' said Aunt Jane.

'Great!' said Ben. 'We can go fishing this afternoon. Dad likes fishing!'

Questions

Chapter 1
1. How old are Ben and Mary?
2. Where do they live? What can they see from their window?
3. What did Ben and Mary get?
4. How did they feel?
5. What can Ben and Mary do?
6. Why did Ben and Mary have to go to the store?
7. What did they buy for Uncle Tom and Aunt Jane?
8. Have you been to the coast?

Chapter 2
1. How did the children get to the coast?
2. Who was on the platform?
3. What was the house like?
4. Where did the children go?
5. What did the children wear? Why?
6. Have you been sailing?
7. Did you wear a life jacket?

Chapter 3
1. What did the children learn?
2. Where did the big boat go?
3. What did Uncle Tom and Aunt Jane do?
4. What was Mr. East like?
5. What did a man do? Why?
6. What time did Mary get up?

7 What did she see?
8 What do you think will happen next?

Chapter 4
1 Where did the man go?
2 Who did the man talk to?
3 What do you think the men are going to do?
4 Who did Ben and Mary pretend to be?
5 Who arrived at the marina?
6 What do you think will happen next?

Chapter 5
1 What did the man do?
2 What did Mary do?
3 What did the sailor do?
4 Who did Uncle Tom phone?
5 Why did the men kidnap Peter?
6 How did Aunt Jane feel?
7 How do you think Mary and Ben's parents felt?
8 What do you think Mr. East will say to Mary?

The Duck and the Kangaroo

Said the Duck to the Kangaroo,
  'Good gracious! how you hop!
Over the fields and the water too,
  As if you never would stop!
My life is a bore in this nasty pond,
And I long to go out in the world beyond!
  I wish I could hop like you!'
  Said the Duck to the Kangaroo.

'Please give me a ride on your back!'
  Said the Duck to the Kangaroo.
'I would sit quite still, and say nothing but *Quack*,
  The whole of the long day through!
And we'd go to the Dee, and the Jelly Bo Lee,
Over the land, and over the sea —
  Please take me a ride![1] O do!'
  Said the Duck to the Kangaroo.

Said the Kangaroo to the Duck,
   'This requires some little reflection[2];
Perhaps on the whole it might bring me luck,
   And there seems but one objection,
Which is, if you'll let me speak so bold,
Your feet are unpleasantly wet and cold,
   And would probably give me the roo-
   Matiz!' said the Kangaroo.

Said the Duck, 'As I sate[3] on the rocks,
   I have thought over that completely,
And I bought four pairs of worsted[4] socks
   Which fit my web-feet neatly.
And to keep out the cold I've bought a cloak[5],
And every day a cigar I'll smoke,
   All to follow my own dear true
   Love of a Kangaroo!'

Said the Kangaroo, 'I'm ready!
   All in the moonlight pale;
But to balance me well, dear Duck, sit steady!
   And quite at the end of my tail!'
And they hopped the whole world three times round
   And who so happy, — O who,
   As the Duck and the Kangaroo?

Edward Lear

1 *take me a ride*   take me for a ride
2 *reflection*   thought
3 *sate*   sat
4 *worsted*   wool
5 *cloak*   a coat with no sleeves

Teevee[1]

In the house
of Mr. and Mrs. Spouse
he and she
would watch teevee
and never a word
between them spoken
until the day
the set was broken.

Then 'How do you do?'
said he to she,
'I don't believe
that we've met yet.
Spouse is my name.
What's yours?' he asked.

'Why, mine's the same!'
said she to he,
'Do you suppose that we could be – ?'

But the set came suddenly right about,
and so they never did find out.
Eve Merriam

1 *Teevee* TV